Animal Lives

THE LIFE OF A HAMSTER

By Jan Feder

Illustrated by Tilman Michalski

CHILDRENS PRESS INTERNATIONAL
CHICAGO

Library of Congress Cataloging in Publication Data

Feder, Jan.
  The life of a hamster.

  (Animal lives)
  Translation of: Der Hamster.
  Summary: Text and drawings describe the
physical characteristics, habits, and
behavior of hamsters.
    1. Hamsters—Juvenile literature.
[1. Hamsters] I. Michalski, Tilman, ill.
II. Title. III. Series.
QL737.R638F4   1982   599.32'33   82-12768
ISBN 0-516-08933-1   AACR2

North American 1982 Edition published
by Regensteiner Publishing Enterprises, Inc.

Copyright © Plenary Publications International (Europe bv),
Original English text copyright © Hutchinson Junior Books 1982

It was a warm spring morning. Hoarder the hamster, his cheek pouches bulging with food, was about to go into his burrow. He never stayed out in broad daylight unless he had to. There were too many animals who wanted to eat him.

3

Once one of these animals got him. Hoarder had been out stuffing some of the spring-sown wheat into his cheeks. He didn't see the buzzard until it was too late.

Hoarder was a brave animal. He would have liked to defend himself. But he was helpless in the big bird's claws. The terrified hamster went stiff, as if he were dead. The buzzard flew to the rock where it usually ate its meals.

As soon as the buzzard put Hoarder's stiff body down, Hoarder suddenly came to life. He reared up, hissing fiercely. He puffed out his cheeks to make himself look bigger. He had once driven off a fox by doing this. Why not a buzzard? The buzzard was so surprised that it moved back and Hoarder escaped.

Hoarder usually lived alone. But one day, Hoarder moved into the territory of a female hamster. He left his scent here. When the two hamsters met they sniffed each other carefully. They both were willing to be friendly but were used to being alone. Suddenly the female hissed and ran away. She came back later.

Hoarder courted the female hamster. He showed off for her and followed her around. Gradually she became friendly. She stopped running away and let Hoarder move into her burrow.

There they mated. But a day or two later the female became very mean. She hissed and drove Hoarder away. Although he was bigger and stronger than she was, Hoarder left.

The female's nest chamber was lined with grass. It was here she had her five babies. They were born hairless and blind. They had grown hair and opened their eyes two weeks after birth. They had started eating grass a week after birth.

The female watched her babies closely. If one strayed from the nest, she quickly brought it back. She held it carefully by the scruff of its neck. But as soon as her babies stopped drinking her milk, the babies left the nest. In fact, they set off to dig burrows of their own when they were only three weeks old.

Meanwhile, Hoarder had gone back to his own burrow and had an unpleasant surprise. Some voles had moved in and taken it over. Hoarder was furious. The voles just managed to get away. Hoarder was angry with himself for not catching one.

Summer rolled by, and Hoarder realized that winter was not far off. He dug some more passages and chambers in his burrow. They were deeper down, away from the cold. He dug earth away with his teeth and forepaws. He used his hind paws to fling dirt out behind him.

When Hoarder's winter burrow was ready, he set to work to fill the storerooms. Tirelessly he went between the nearby wheat field and the burrow. Then one day he heard a roaring sound. The farmer was cutting and threshing his crop.

Hoarder raced back to his burrow. He did not dare go back to the field until the farmer had gone.

Then he was running to and fro again, stuffing his pouches with grain and carrying it back to his storerooms.

It was hard work. Sometimes Hoarder was carrying so much that he could scarcely move. Many of the grainfields had been harvested now. Hoarder had to go farther and farther to find food. He was an easy catch for his enemies when he was outside his burrow, but there was no stopping him.

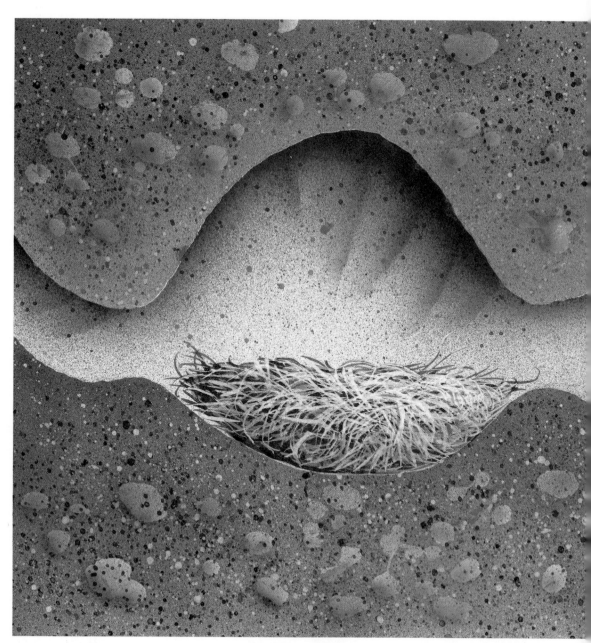

At last his storerooms were full. He could be sure he would not starve during the winter. It was already cold outside. Icy winds whistled over the fields and the meadows.

But as long as he could, Hoarder left his burrow to find his daily food.

At last it was time for Hoarder to hibernate. He blocked up the entrances to his burrow. He curled up in his grass-lined nest. His body became almost cold, and he fell asleep. He would wake up every few days to eat. But he would not go outside again for three or four months, until the warm spring weather came again.

The Hamster

A creature of the steppes

Common hamsters, also known as black-bellied hamsters, originally lived in the treeless plains, or steppes, of eastern Europe. They fed mainly on the seeds of wild grasses growing on the great plains. When people came and learned to grow grain crops, hamsters left their native homes. Soon they lived all over the continent of Europe. Hamsters had found out that eating grain, such as wheat, oats, rye, and barley, was better than eating wild grass seeds.

In parts of western Europe, hamsters became so numerous that they were considered pests because of the damage they did to crops. Today, however, there are not many wild hamsters. They do not live wild in Britain or the United States.

How it lives

The hamster is one of the mouse-like or "murine" group of rodents. It belongs to the family of burrowing rodents whose scientific Latin name is Cricetidae. Its most important tools are its paws and its rodent teeth. Its teeth grow all the time and are worn down by daily use.

The hamster likes to live where the summers are warm and dry. Hamsters dislike rain. Heavy rainfall can be dangerous as it may flood their burrows.

The hamster lives alone in its burrow. It never goes far from its home—unless it can no longer find food nearby. Then it has to look for a new place to find food. Like many mammals, the hamster marks its territory by leaving scent marks. The scent comes from a gland on its flank. The hamster rubs its sides against the spots it wants to mark. Males and females live in the same burrow only at mating time. Then they generally both move into the female's burrow. But the honeymoon never lasts long. Shortly after mating the female becomes bad-tempered and chases the male away.

The hamster is what is called a "crepuscular" animal. That means it is most active in the dusk. It does not normally leave its burrow until twilight—although it may sometimes be forced by hunger to look for food in the daytime.

Out in the open, many dangers threaten the hamster. Its natural enemies are birds of prey, such as the buzzard by day and the owl by night. Some animals, such as martens, weasels, polecats, foxes, and stray dogs, are enemies. If the hamster has no hope of escape it will stand and defend itself bravely. It quite often comes off the winner.

The male hamster is a sturdy little animal. He grows to a length of up to 12 inches (30 centimeters), his tail is another 2 inches (5 centimeters) long. He weighs up to 18 pounds (500 grams). The female, on the other hand, is smaller. The hamster has a piebald coat. Its belly is dark, and the animal uses it to impress an enemy when it rears up on its hind legs to threaten or attack.

Hamsters hibernate through winter and early spring. They retire to their burrows and block up the entrances. Then the hamster's body cools down. Its temperature sinks from 89.6 degrees Fahrenheit (32 degrees Celcius) to 39 to 41 degrees Fahrenheit (4 or 5 degrees Celcius), and it begins hibernating. However, hibernation is interrupted. About once every five to seven days the hamster wakes up in order to eat.

The hamster and its burrow

The hamster digs its own burrow with its teeth and paws. It uses its front paws and teeth to scrape earth up and bite through roots. It pushes the loose earth away with its hind paws.

Its summer burrow usually has a storeroom and a nest chamber which the hamster lines with grass, feathers, and other soft stuff. It also has a tunnel that it uses as a lavatory. The hamster is a very clean animal. Its burrow usually has several entrances. There is a dead-end hole near the entrance into which the hamster can fall in times of danger.

It extends its burrow for the winter by adding another storeroom and another nest chamber. When the hamster begins to hibernate, it blocks up all the entrances to the burrow. The hamster will hoard food in its storerooms at any time of year,

Features of the Hamster

Scent gland on flank

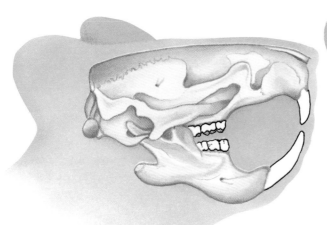

Side view of skull, showing teeth

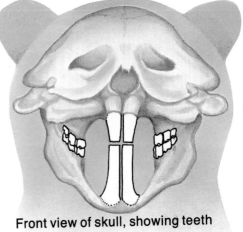

Front view of skull, showing teeth

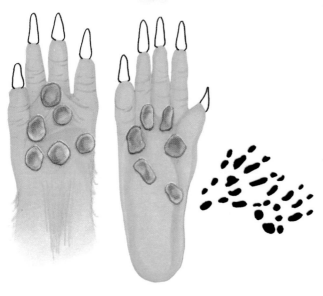

Forepaw   Hind paw

Tracks made by a
hamster moving slowly

just in case of an emergency. But it lays in particularly large stores for the winter. Up to 100 pounds of grain have been found in a hamster's burrow.

There are dangers lying in wait for the hamster everywhere outside the burrow. So it stuffs everything edible into its cheek pouches. It gathers food in this way so busily that it has become a symbol of greed in the countries where it lives wild. Back in its burrow, the hamster strokes its cheeks with both front paws until the pouches are empty again.

The hamster is mainly a vegetarian, living on plants. But it will sometimes eat small creatures such as worms, snails, and beetles, and even voles and tree frogs.

Courtship

If a male wants to mate, he will make his way boldly into a female's territory. He will mark it with his own scent (it will already be marked with hers), as a warning to rivals to keep out. When he first meets the female, the two hamsters sniff each other briefly. They are normally solitary animals. So the female usually

hisses angrily at the male and runs away. But she comes back again, and the game is repeated. Gradually she runs more and more slowly, so that the male can catch up with her. During his courtship he makes a soft snuffling noise. He also grinds his teeth to impress the female. He grinds his teeth in the same way to frighten off rivals.

Mating

Mating takes place in the female hamster's burrow, when the male has settled in. The female throws him out again afterwards. Although he is stronger than she, he goes meekly. He probably has some idea that the female will have her young now.

The litter is born about eighteen to twenty days after mating. A female hamster has two litters a year. Each litter generally contains four to eight babies, occasionally more. Only eight of a large litter will survive because the mother has not enough teats to suckle more. (Any remaining young will therefore either die of hunger or be eaten by their mother. This is simply the working of a natural law.)

How the Hamster Carries Food

Biting off a leaf

Getting the leaf into position

Stuffing the leaf into its cheek pouches

Emptying the cheek pouches

The Hamster's Burrow

Summer burrow:

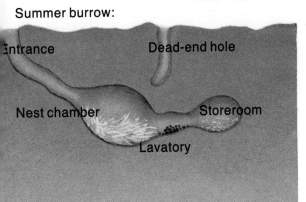

Entrance

Dead-end hole

Nest chamber

Storeroom

Lavatory

Winter burrow:

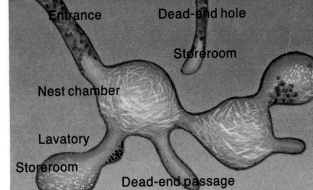

Entrance

Dead-end hole

Storeroom

Nest chamber

Lavatory

Storeroom

Dead-end passage

The Hamster and its Relations

(Cricetidae family)

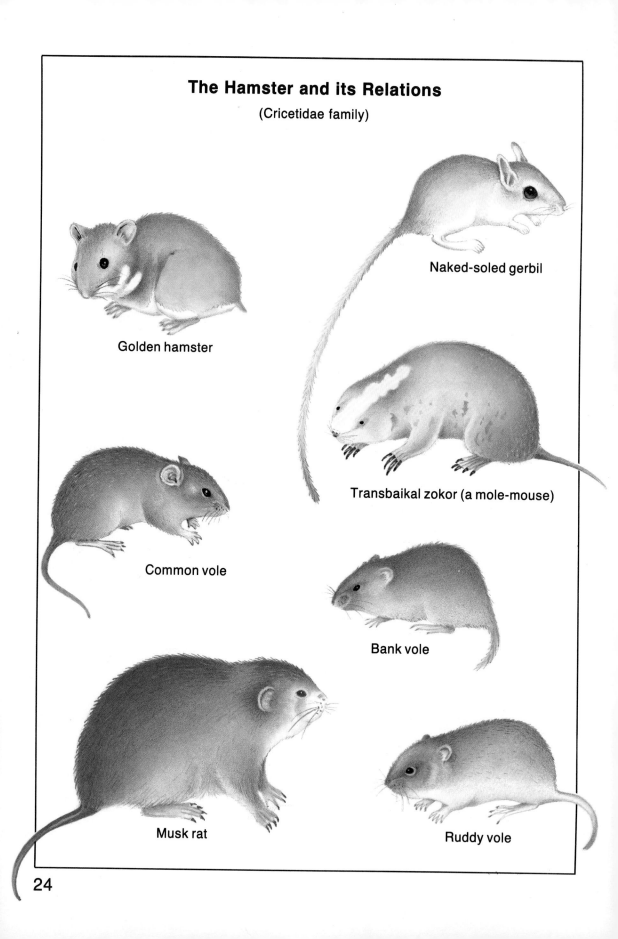

Naked-soled gerbil

Golden hamster

Transbaikal zokor (a mole-mouse)

Common vole

Bank vole

Musk rat

Ruddy vole

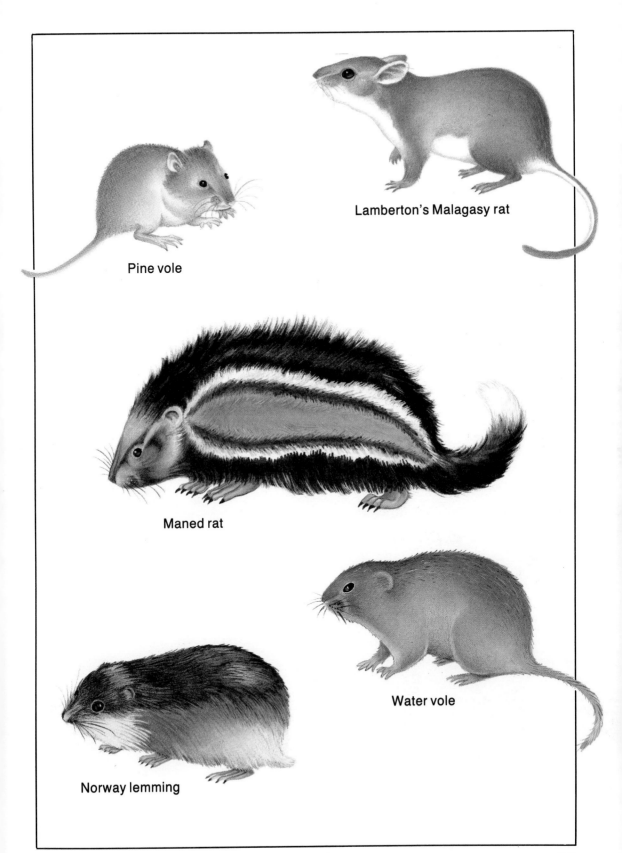

Lamberton's Malagasy rat

Pine vole

Maned rat

Water vole

Norway lemming

The young are born blind and hairless. They do not open their eyes until they are two weeks old. By then they have grown hair. But the baby hamsters begin to eat grass when they are only a week old. Although they are still blind at that point, they can find their own way from the nest to the storeroom. Once they can see, they will often crawl to the entrance of the burrow and have to be fetched back by their mother. She takes them carefully by the scruff of the neck, and they immediately go stiff. This rigid posture is typical of a hamster being carried.

After about three weeks, they finally stop suckling and leave the burrow to become independent. Now they dig their own burrows. A small hamster may be seen above ground, not making its way determinedly in one direction—which would be towards its burrow—but scurrying to and fro as if at a loss, or even perhaps squaring up to fight. It is sure to be a young animal who has not yet dug its own burrow. A hamster is fully grown at about eight weeks.

Fighting

When the hamster hears any suspicious noise it sits up and takes notice. It rears halfway up and remains quite still on its hindquarters for a few seconds. If it is aware of danger nearby, it quickly makes for safety. If it cannot escape, it faces its enemy. It rears right up on its hind legs with its forepaws raised in front of it or spread out. It puffs out its cheek pouches to make itself look bigger and more impressive. It hisses loudly, threatening its enemy, bares its teeth, and grinds them together.

At first it will only make mock attacks, jumping backward and forward. But if that does not scare the enemy off, it attacks in earnest, leaping rapidly at the enemy and biting. The hamster can inflict quite deep and nasty wounds with its lower incisors. It makes the same sort of mock attacking movements when what it really wants to do is escape. The enemy will flinch slightly at each attacking movement, and this allows the hamster itself to retreat a little farther back. If it is pursued, it repeats its mock attack, until it has reached a hole into which it can slip.

Two Male Hamsters Fighting

Sniffing each other

Threatening

Attacking the opponent's belly

Both on the attack

A successful bite

The loser goes away

However, if a hamster meets a rival, the fight follows different rules (look at the illustrations on page 27). First, the two hamsters run at each other. They threaten one another by grinding their teeth and sniffing each other over, sometimes moving round in circles. Then they rear up face to face, hissing and squealing, until one hamster suddenly attacks. Like many other rodents, hamsters go for each other's flanks. As the enemy hamster is not likely to stand still and do nothing, both animals will soon be clinched in a tangled ball. When they let go of each other after a few seconds, the weaker hamster may be ready to run away. If he is followed, which is what usually happens, he tries to shake off his pursuer by dodging sideways. However, if the other hamster does catch up with him, he will throw himself down on his back, with his forepaws spread out, and squeal loudly. After this gesture of surrender he will not be bitten hard. This is roughly the course of a battle between male hamsters competing for a female. In a fight over territory, the occupant often attacks the intruder without warning, so violently that the other hamster has to run for it.

What happens, however, when a hamster has to fight and his cheek pouches are full? The answer is that, sorry as he may be to lose his meal, he quickly empties the pouches in order to be ready for battle. He cannot hiss impressively with his mouth full!

A clean animal
Like many small mammals, the hamster likes to groom itself, usually when it is safe inside its burrow. It usually begins by washing its head and face, and then, in a sitting position, grooms its chest and belly, and then its sides and its hind paws.

The Hamster's Body Language

Crouching. The hamster feels at ease, and not threatened

Hamster washing. First it moistens its paws

On the alert. The hamster is curious about something

Then it begins washing, cleaning its mouth and eyes first

Hamster rearing up ready to attack

Finally it cleans the back of its neck

Interesting Facts about the Hamster

Man and the common hamster

European farmers do not like hamsters. They often damage the roots of crops when they dig their burrows. Also, although they are more or less omnivorous and will eat mice and other small vermin, they really prefer crops like alfalfa and grain. In some years, when hamsters have bred particularly well, they have endangered the whole harvest. A hamster may hoard up to 100 pounds of food as its winter store. If there are several hamsters in a field the farmer loses a lot of his harvest. Farmers plagued by hamsters in Europe used to dig up the animals' burrows before the winter set in to

recover the stored food, which could still be used as cattle fodder, or even when it was mostly grain, for baking bread .

One group of hamsters is said to have left its Russian home after a drought and emigrated. Apparently they even crossed a wide river, where many of them drowned. But in the end they reached Rumania. At first they hid under fishermen's boats and then came out at night to make their way into the villages. This plague of hamsters in Rumania did so much damage that it was proclaimed every farmer's duty to kill fifty. There have been years where money rewards were offered for the killing of hamsters in Germany—for instance, just after World War II.

The hamster's fur

Furriers, as well as farmers, are among the hamster's human enemies. Fur coats can be made out of the little animals' skins.

The hamster as food

In a game law of Augustus the Strong, King of Prussia and Elector of Saxony in the early eighteenth century, the hamster is mentioned as being small game. However, though it may have been hunted as game, no recipes for cooking hamsters have actually come down to us!

The golden hamster

The well-known Syrian golden hamster is a relative of the common hamster. Its short recorded history is a very strange one. An English explorer called Waterhouse discovered the golden hamster in the Syrian desert in 1839. He gave a precise description of the animal. He also brought back a specimen skin. After that, no more was heard of the golden hamster, and it seemed to have died out.

However, in 1930, almost a hundred years later, a female golden hamster with twelve young was dug up by Professor Aharoni at

Aleppo in Syria. They were found in a burrow 2.7 yards (2.3 meters) underground. The Syrian golden hamster has never again been found living free in the wild. All the golden hamsters that are now favorite household pets for children throughout the world are descended from this one litter. Professor Aharoni raised a hundred and fifty young hamsters in the first year. One female had litters of first six, then eight, and then twelve young. In 1931 the first live golden hamsters arrived in England. Seven years after that they were exported to America. They did not become popular pets until after World War II.

Originally, the golden hamster was always golden brown in color with a white belly. But breeding has produced varieties that are gray, blue, white, beige, multicolored, and piebald. Sometimes one may see hamsters bred to look like pugs or boxer dogs. It is amazing to think that all these varieties have been bred from one desert animal!

Keeping golden hamsters as pets

There are millions of golden hamsters in the world, all kept as pets. All are descended from the single female and her young dug up by Professor Aharoni. With their button eyes and cuddly look, these little animals are favorites with children. But they are not really cage animals. They need an enormous amount of exercise daily. It is essential to have a wheel in a golden hamster's cage. They need to be on the move for at least six hours a day—or rather,

six hours a night, since golden hamsters are definitely nocturnal animals, more so than the crepuscular (twilight waking) common hamsters. The golden hamster is really a long-distance runner of great stamina. However, golden hamsters cannot be allowed to run loose around the home. They will eat anything that is not firmly fastened down. One reason against keeping golden hamsters as pets for children is that they live for only two to four years. Some varieties have a lifespan of only one year. That means that children lose their pets after a relatively short time. Golden hamsters kept in pairs will breed rapidly, having young up to ten times a year. Then one is faced with the problem of finding homes for all the babies.

Characteristics of the golden hamster

The golden hamster, in the wild, lives in burrows in the desert, and is nocturnal (wakes at night). This means that it likes to be left in peace during the day, and to run around and dig a great deal at night.

It can start having young of its own when it is four weeks old. Its pregnancy lasts 16 to 18 days and it may have up to 15 babies in a litter, each weighing about .07 ounces (2 grams). They are blind for the first ten days, and their mother suckles them for about three weeks.

Index